CW01433651

Original title:
Hazel Strips Among the Witch Loop

Copyright © 2025 Swan Charm
All rights reserved.

Twinkling Midnight in Haunting Woods

Underneath the moon's pale light,
Shadows flicker, take their flight.
Whispers curl through ancient trees,
Brought by night on playful breeze.

Twinkling stars in velvet sky,
Guard the dreams that flutter by.
Echoes of the past resound,
In the woods where magic's found.

Footsteps soft on mossy ground,
In this realm, lost souls are found.
Lurking sprites with laughter bright,
Guide the lost through endless night.

Every path a secret keeps,
Where the wild and wonder sleeps.
Time stands still in twilight's grace,
Mysteries in every space.

Flashes of a fleeting dream,
Dancing in the moonlit beam.
With each breath, the forest sighs,
As the midnight magic flies.

The Dance of the Wayward Wind

Across the hills, the warm winds play,
Chasing clouds that drift away.
In the glen, the flowers sway,
As if they're joining in the fray.

Invisible a tune they hum,
Echoing like a distant drum.
Dancing leaves, a lively dance,
Inviting all to take a chance.

Through the eaves, the breezes rush,
In the twilight, feelings flush.
Whispers of forgotten tales,
Ride the wind on evening gales.

From the mountains to the sea,
Carrying each heart set free.
Yearning for a world unknown,
With every gust, new seeds are sown.

Beneath the stars, a journey calls,
The wayward wind through shadows falls.
Join the dance, embrace the night,
With every breath, behold the light.

Gossamer Dreams in Twilight

In the hush of dusk's embrace,
Where shadows gently sway,
Whispers of long-lost tales,
Awake the night's ballet.

Gossamer threads of time,
Weave through the dusky air,
Stars peek through velvet clouds,
In twilight's dreamlike lair.

A soft sigh of secrets,
Lingers where wishes dwell,
Bathed in the moon's soft glow,
Each heart knows its spell.

Ancient trees stand guard,
Roots deep in the earth's song,
While crickets play a tune,
For the dreamers who belong.

Underneath this mystic sky,
Hope flutters, wild and free,
In gossamer dreams of twilight,
Where souls find their decree.

When the Witches Gather

In the heart of the forest deep,
Beneath the crescent moon,
Witches whisper ancient spells,
Their laughter like a tune.

Cloaks of midnight fabric weave,
As shadows twirl and sway,
With herbs and potions brewing,
They beckon night to play.

Candles flicker in the breeze,
Casting shapes on the ground,
Secrets binding, hands entwined,
An echoing magic sound.

Around the cauldron's edge they dance,
With mystic words and signs,
When the witches gather close,
The universe entwines.

Every spell a story spun,
Every laugh a light,
In the sacred circle of night,
They conjure dreams in flight.

Tangles of Gold and Silver

In the glen where sunlight beams,
And shadows softly glide,
Whispers weave through golden grass,
Where secrets choose to hide.

Silver streams glisten bright,
Reflecting tales of old,
Every ripple sings of time,
In tangles wrought of gold.

Willow branches bow and sway,
Guardians of the past,
As winds of change seek solace,
In memories held fast.

Flowers bloom in colors rare,
Their petals soft and bold,
In the fabric of the earth,
Tangles of love unfold.

Beneath the whispered evening sky,
With dreams of ages spun,
Life entwines in beauty's grasp,
As twilight's work is done.

The Sylvan Veil of Secrets

In the heart of ancient woods,
Where sunlight dares to creep,
A sylvan veil of secrets sways,
In whispers soft as sleep.

Mossy carpets welcome all,
With shadows long and deep,
Each step reveals a hidden path,
Where nature's treasures keep.

Elusive creatures flit and fade,
In the dappled light they play,
Guardians of forgotten lore,
That twilight holds at bay.

The air is thick with magic,
As silence sings its tune,
Underneath the watchful boughs,
By the silver crescent moon.

In this realm where secrets live,
And wonders gently blend,
The sylvan veil invites your heart,
To seek and never end.

The Hidden Cauldron Beneath the Roots

In shadows deep where whispers dwell,
A cauldron hides beneath the swell.
Roots entwine, a tangled mesh,
Guarding secrets, ancient flesh.

Silent spells in earthen clay,
Guarded by the night and day.
Brews of magic, potion's flight,
Stirred by dreams in deepest night.

The moonlight dances on the ground,
Echoes of a time profound.
With each heartbeat, echoes call,
From hidden depths where shadows fall.

The air is thick with shimmering spark,
As lanterns glow, igniting dark.
A riddle lies within the steam,
Unraveling the forgotten dream.

In whispered winds, the truth concealed,
A story waits, yet to be revealed.
By roots entwined, we seek the lore,
Of potions brewed and worlds before.

Fables of the Frosted Ferns

Upon the hills where fronds arise,
A tale is stitched in silver ties.
Frosted leaves like whispers sway,
Guarding secrets of the day.

In winter's grasp, the magic stirs,
Each breath a hymn, the icy purrs.
Beneath their boughs, the fables grow,
Of lost enchantments, tales of woe.

Beneath the snow, the stories sleep,
In nature's arms, their vigil keep.
When spring awakens from its slumber,
Frolic and dance, let hearts encumber.

The frost will yield, the sun will shine,
Revealing paths where stars align.
With each fresh bloom, the stories weave,
A tapestry of dreams believe.

Fables spun in misty breath,
A cycle born from life and death.
In every fern, a whisper sings,
Of magic rare, and wondrous things.

A Journey Through the Silken Glade

Through silken paths where shadows flow,
A journey waits for hearts in tow.
The glade enfolds with gentle grace,
A tapestry of time and space.

With every step, the silence hums,
In harmony, the soft wind drums.
The trees entwine with tales they hold,
Of ancient truths and moments bold.

Glimmers of light like fireflies play,
Guiding wanderers on their way.
Each breath a spark, each glance a dream,
In nature's weave, the stars do gleam.

The silk threads shimmer with a glow,
Whispering secrets only few know.
In every rustle, a story breathes,
In every sigh, a magic weaves.

As dusk descends in twilight's hue,
The glade awakes to life anew.
In shadows deep, the spirits call,
To join the dance, to lose it all.

Ephemeral Glimpses of Celestial Beings

In twilight's veil where dreams unfold,
Celestial beings, secrets told.
They flit like stars, in paths unknown,
Whispering tales on winds that moan.

With every shimmer, realms collide,
Bridging worlds with swift, soft glide.
Ephemeral dances, bright and rare,
Glimpses of magic linger in the air.

Their laughter echoes through the night,
A radiant glow, a wondrous sight.
In the hush of dusk, where spirits play,
They beckon us to join the sway.

As morning breaks, the visions fade,
Yet memories of their light cascade.
Each fleeting moment, pure and sweet,
Carved in time, an endless beat.

In heart and mind, their whispers stay,
Like gentle dreams that never fray.
In every star, their essence gleams,
Ephemeral glimpses, woven dreams.

Whispers of the Enchanted Grove

In the grove where shadows play,
Whispers dance on leaves at bay,
Secrets linger on the breeze,
Nature's heart, a gentle tease.

Moonlight spills on forest deep,
Guarded dreams and whispers keep,
Through the brambles, soft and light,
Magic glimmers in the night.

Ancient tales in roots entwined,
Magic threads that fate designed,
Every rustle, every sigh,
Carries stars across the sky.

With each footstep, time stands still,
Beneath the oak, where spirits thrill,
In the stillness, voices rise,
Calling softly, wise and wise.

Swaying branches, secrets told,
In shadows deep, the brave and bold,
Treading paths of whispered lore,
The grove, a realm forevermore.

Secrets Woven in Twilight's Loom

In twilight's grip, the world unfolds,
A tapestry of stories told,
Threads of gold in dusky air,
Binding dreams with gentle care.

Stars awake, their secrets twine,
Each shimmering spark, a sacred sign,
Weaving light in the dusky veil,
Where whispers linger, soft and frail.

A raven's cry, a distant call,
Echoes through the evening hall,
Nature's breath, a silent song,
Invisible threads binding strong.

In shadows cast by inky night,
Gentle spirits take their flight,
Underneath the silver moon,
They dance to nature's ancient tune.

Through the darkness, magic stirs,
A world alive, a symphony of furs,
Secrets breathed in twilight's loom,
Awakening wonders from the gloom.

The Dance of Twilight Shadows

Twilight steals the day away,
Shadows stretch and dance at play,
With every flicker, night's embrace,
Brings a stillness, a soft grace.

Moonbeams shimmer on the ground,
As whispers weave around and round,
In the dusk's gentle hold we find,
Memories left far behind.

Leaves rustle with ancient glee,
In this night, we're wild and free,
Every heartbeat, every sigh,
Echoes softly through the sky.

Figures glide in twilight's thrall,
Casting spells—a soft enthrall,
With every turn, a story spun,
In the silence, dreams begun.

Hold your breath, the night is young,
In twilight's dance, hearts are strung,
Secrets whispered, shadows sway,
As stars awaken, night holds sway.

Threads of Nature's Mystique

Nature spins a woven dream,
Through hushed forests and silver stream,
Threads of green and earthy browns,
Crafting beauty all around.

With a whisper, petals fall,
Every moment, a timeless call,
In the fabric of the wild,
Lies the mystery of the child.

With dewdrops kissed by morning light,
Nature's wonder takes its flight,
On each branch, on every leaf,
Lives the essence, pure belief.

Winding paths, a gentle trace,
Every turn, a new embrace,
In the silence, secrets bloom,
In nature's dance, we find our room.

Threads of magic, old and new,
Binding hearts as dreams come true,
Within the arms of mystique's reign,
We find solace, we find gain.

Whirling Fables of the Woodlands

In the heart of the forest, whispers play,
With every turn, the stories sway.
Fables weave through the mossy ground,
In this realm where magic is found.

The brook sings secrets, soft and low,
While ancient trees in twilight glow.
Adventurers tread where fairies gleam,
Chasing the edge of a woodland dream.

Flickers of light dance in the shade,
Each corner hides the charms they've made.
With laughter echoing, joy takes flight,
As night drapes gently, cloaked in night.

Beneath the boughs where shadows play,
A tapestry of night and day.
With every tale, the heart shall soar,
Whirling fables forevermore.

Where Spirits Whisper Among the Leaves

In the rustle of leaves, a story calls,
Among the branches, enchantment falls.
Spirits linger where silence keeps,
Guardians watch while the woodland sleeps.

Old oaks murmur with wisdom deep,
Secrets of the forest, theirs to keep.
With every breeze, a soft refrain,
Awakens the magic in the rain.

Beneath the stars, the shadows flit,
Where ethereal dancers often sit.
In twilight's glow, their laughter blends,
As nature's tale unfolds, transcends.

Listen closely, for voices hum,
In the heart of the woodlands, spirits come.
They weave their tales in the gentle night,
Where whispering winds share their delight.

Constellations Beneath the Canopy

Under the canopy, the stars arise,
Hidden wonders in velvet skies.
Constellations dance with a radiant glow,
In the embrace of magic, time moves slow.

Fireflies twinkle, a nebulous flight,
Guiding the dreamers through the night.
As branches sway, celestial sights,
Hold the stories of forgotten nights.

In secret glades, the moonlight weaves,
A tapestry where the heart believes.
Echoes of laughter, soft and clear,
Shimmer like stardust, rich and dear.

Each breath of night a spell to cast,
In the woodland's cradle, shadows vast.
Constellations pulse in harmony bright,
Beneath the leaves where dreams take flight.

Shadows of Incantation and Delight

In the shadows where secrets dwell,
Incantations weave a timeless spell.
With whispered words and ancient lore,
The heart of the woodlands opens its door.

Winds carry murmurs of spells untold,
Through valleys deep and forests old.
Beneath the boughs, the magic streams,
Filling the night with enchanting dreams.

Each flicker of light, a sign to heed,
Where nature's wonders plant the seed.
In twilight's embrace, the world ignites,
With shadows dancing in the moon's light.

In every rustle, a tale unfolds,
As the woodland whispers, brave and bold.
With laughter mingling in the night,
Shadows of incantation and delight.

Rooted in the Enigma of the Wildwood

In the heart of the whispering trees,
Beneath a canopy thick with dreams,
Ancient roots entwine like secrets,
Guarding tales forgotten in streams.

Moonlight dances on mossy floors,
Casting shadows that twist and twine,
Each step taken on the old path,
Is a promise whispered, a sign.

Creatures stir in twilight's embrace,
With eyes like lanterns, glowing bright,
They hold the keys to mysteries,
Held close by the softness of night.

Ephemeral ferns sway gently proud,
In a ballet only they can know,
A symphony sung by the wild,
As time softly ebbs and flows.

Here magic lingers, unseen by most,
In the wildwood's tender caress,
Each leaf a reminder, each breeze a host,
Of the enigma that we all possess.

Whimsies Lurking Beneath the Green Veil

Beneath the arch of emerald hues,
Whimsies frolic in dappled light,
Where daisies whisper, secrets muse,
And shadows play with hearts so bright.

Glimmers of laughter dance on the air,
As the brook sings her lilting tune,
Awakening dreams from slumber's lair,
Under the watch of a gentle moon.

Each fluttering leaf tells a story,
Of creatures hiding away from sight,
With threads of hope woven in glory,
In the embrace of the midnights bright.

The fox spins tales of the night fox-light,
While the old oak groans in the breeze,
As faeries sprinkle their stardust bright,
On the flowers that bloom with ease.

Oh, to wander where whimsy finds,
Its delicate dance in the sigh of night,
Where imaginations soar and bind,
In a world cloaked in shades of might.

The Glade of Forgotten Whispers

In a glade where the silence speaks,
Whispers wrap 'round the ancient stones,
Echoing memories of the weak,
And tales of lost hearts and forlorn.

The wind carries secrets untold,
Through thickets that weave with grace,
Stories of dreams that once were bold,
Now linger in time's hidden space.

Ferns curl shyly, protecting the past,
Where shadows lap and light seeks to play,
In this haven, the moments last,
As twilight blurs the edge of day.

A lantern bird sings its low tune,
While crickets nod, an evening cheer,
Softly urging the rise of the moon,
In the glade where lost whispers steer.

Each breath taken, a brush with fate,
As echoes merge in twilight's flow,
In the heart of the glade, we await,
The secrets only the stars know.

Dreams Bound by Silken Vines

In the twilight where visions twine,
Dreams hang heavy in the air,
Bound by silken threads divine,
Weaving stories, beyond compare.

Each twilight bloom unfurls its gift,
As night drapes velvet on the grove,
Whispers of wishes begin to drift,
Where the becomes the heart's cove.

Beneath the starlit tapestry wide,
A journey beckons, soft and near,
In the shadows, where hopes reside,
And every longing whispers clear.

As the moon weaves tales of silver light,
The vines entwine with dreams unreal,
Cradling wishes, gentle and bright,
Leaving echoes for hearts to feel.

So wander softly, lost in thought,
For the night holds secrets profound,
In every thread carefully wrought,
Dreams take flight, forever unbound.

Luminous Pathways Through the Thicket

In shadows deep, where whispers creep,
A golden glow begins to seep.
Each step we take, on winding trails,
The light around us gently hails.

Amidst the ferns, in dew-kissed air,
We trace the secrets hidden there.
The ancient trees with branches wide,
Guard stories of the world inside.

Upon the path where moonbeams dance,
A flicker's spark ignites our trance.
We follow paths where dreams align,
And wander through the thickened pine.

With every turn, a new surprise,
The magic glows, ignites our eyes.
Soft echoes of the past reside,
In luminescent truth we glide.

So here we'll roam, where wild hearts beat,
On luminous pathways we repeat.
The thicket's gift, a guiding light,
Leads us through day and into night.

Enigmas Woven in Twine

In twilight's hold, where shadows loom,
We find the strands that chase the gloom.
Knots of riddles hang like breath,
While whispers dance with hints of death.

A tapestry of threads so fine,
Woven secrets twist and twine.
Each flicker hints at tales untold,
Of mystic realms and treasures gold.

Beneath the stars, a cipher plays,
Unraveling through starlit bays.
With gentle hands, we tread the wane,
As sunlight shifts, and dusk regains.

Threads will guide through paths unknown,
A quest for hearts once lost, alone.
We'll puzzle out, with minds entwined,
The enigmas woven, all aligned.

So let us tread on this fine line,
And dance with fate, our spirits shine.
For in the dark, what calls us forth,
Are mysteries wrapped in twine of worth.

The Dance of Starlit Branches

In evening's breath, the branches sway,
With every pulse, they twirl and play.
Their silhouettes 'gainst twilight's hue,
Compose a dance that feels so true.

Above us shine the nighttime's grace,
With twinkling lights, they weave and trace.
Each spectral flicker, a dancer's flair,
As if the cosmos knows we're there.

Together caught in nature's song,
The whispers of the night are strong.
We lose ourselves in soft allure,
Each step we take feels rich and pure.

Along the boughs, soft shadows glide,
An endless dance where souls confide.
In harmony, we find our chance,
Entranced, we join the branches' dance.

With every twirl, a fleeting glance,
We bridge the gap, we take the chance.
In starlit night, where dreams are spun,
A dance begins, as hearts are one.

Echoes of the Eldritch Woods

In twilight's clamor, woods awake,
With echoes that the stillness shake.
The whispers rise from roots so deep,
A haunting hymn that stirs from sleep.

The trees stand guard, their secrets old,
In shadows cast, the tales unfold.
With every breeze that brushes by,
The stories stretch and never die.

Through tangled vines, the shadows creep,
In every sound, a promise keep.
The eldritch woods, with eyes so wide,
Invite the lost to come inside.

Beneath the boughs, where dreams confound,
Integrity of magic found.
With echoes clear, we pave the way,
Through mysteries where moonlight stays.

So join the dance, let voices blend,
In echoes where the tales descend.
In eldritch woods, we find our peace,
A bond with shadows, a sweet release.

Enchanted Echoes from the Forest Floor

Whispers linger in the shades,
Softly spoken, serenades.
Mossy carpets, secrets spun,
Breathe the magic, feel the fun.

Amidst the ferns, a dance of light,
Twirling shadows, calm and bright.
Footsteps echo, hearts align,
Every pulse feels so divine.

Murmurs rise from hidden streams,
Flowing softly through our dreams.
Nature's song, a timeless lore,
Echoes darting, evermore.

Glimmers of the past unfold,
Stories waiting to be told.
Each rustling leaf, a tale of old,
In the forest, wonders bold.

A tapestry of green and gold,
In the heart, magic untold.
Brightened paths beneath the trees,
Here, the spirit finds its ease.

Light Trapped in the Canopy's Grasp

Sunbeams filter, golden rays,
Dancing gently through the haze.
Leaves of emerald catch the fire,
Nature's breath, a heart's desire.

Nutmeg whispers, spices blend,
Swaying branches, softly bend.
In this realm where shadows play,
Light and dark weave night and day.

Sparrows flit, a sudden thrill,
Moments pause, then time stands still.
Beneath the boughs, a world ensnares,
Where every dream and thought repairs.

Hushed enchantments in the air,
Secrets linger everywhere.
With each step, the silence sings,
Of timeless joys that nature brings.

Caught in webs, both bright and rare,
Dreams entwined with gentle care.
Through the leaves, the stories swirl,
In the canopy, magic's pearl.

The Spell of the Starlit Wilderness

Underneath the vast night sky,
Stars awaken, softly sigh.
Moonlight drapes with silver thread,
Casting dreams where footsteps tread.

A velvet cloak of darkened hue,
Whispers ancient secrets, true.
Creatures stir and shadows glide,
In this haven, hopes abide.

Twinkling lights, a cosmic sea,
Carved from time's infinity.
Mysterious paths that bend and weave,
In this dream, we dare believe.

Echoes of a wizard's song,
Guide the lost where they belong.
In the silent wood, hearts soar,
The wilderness calls forevermore.

A dance of fireflies brings delight,
In the embracing arms of night.
With every twinkle, magic lives,
The wilderness, our spirit gives.

Beneath the Veils of Time's Enchantment

Ancient trees with stories write,
Branching out through day and night.
Every knot a whisper shared,
In their presence, hearts have bared.

Time, a river flowing fast,
Moments caught, yet shadows cast.
Beneath the bark, a world aglow,
In silence, secrets freely flow.

The past and present intertwine,
A tapestry of fate divine.
With every breath, the echoes call,
In time's embrace, we rise and fall.

Brightened by the dusk's sweet hue,
Memories brush the heart anew.
In the twilight's soft caress,
We glean the magic, feel the blessed.

Through the mists that gently dance,
Time unveils its mystic chance.
Beneath the veils, we find our place,
In the forest's tight embrace.

Echoes Through the Witching Woods

In shadows deep where whispers twine,
The crooked branches form a sign.
With secrets hushed and breezes low,
The ancient magic starts to flow.

A lantern glows, the path reveals,
The echo of forgotten feels.
Through tangled roots and misty air,
The heart of night begins to stare.

A fae's dance caught in moonlit weave,
Where spirits sigh and hearts believe.
Each step unfolds a story's thread,
In twilight's grip, the past is fed.

The owls hoot tales of those who roamed,
Through time and space, they've always combed.
With every turn, the forest breathes,
A symphony of twilight leaves.

So tread with care, dear wanderer brave,
For in this wood, there's magic to save.
Embrace the echoes, feel the lure,
For in your heart, the woods endure.

Moonlit Paths of Forgotten Lore

Upon the hill where shadows gleam,
A silver path leads to a dream.
Where starlit skies weave ancient tales,
And wisdom rides on gentle gales.

In glades where secrets softly hide,
By stone and stream, the echoes bide.
Each whispered thought a tale retold,
Of lives once lived, of truths so bold.

The moon, a lantern hangs so high,
Illuminates the magic nigh.
As crickets sing their serenade,
Through whispered woods, the night parade.

In every rustle, every sound,
The mysteries of night abound.
Take heed, dear soul, within the night,
The dance of lore will bring you light.

So walk the paths where stories weave,
And breathe the air, allow, believe.
For every step be filled with grace,
In moonlit woods, find your place.

Where Sorcery Meets Sylvan Tapestry

In glimmering glades where wonders bloom,
The forest hums a vibrant tune.
From whispered winds to dancing leaves,
The essence of the magic weaves.

Here sorcerers tread with softest wings,
In harmony with nature's strings.
Among the roots where fairies flit,
Their laughter echoes, spirits lit.

With every step on mossy ground,
The threads of fate in silence wound.
Through ancient trees and scent of pine,
A tapestry of fate divine.

Mysteries glow in twilight's breath,
Life whispers softly, but not in death.
For here, in realms where magic sings,
The heart knows well what wonder brings.

So pause and ponder, breathe it in,
The sorcery that lies within.
For in each glance, a world anew,
Where sylvan tales will beckon you.

Enigmas Nestled in Verdant Veils

In emerald shrouds where secrets dwell,
The forest holds its cryptic spell.
With every leaf that rustles near,
An enigma whispers, soft but clear.

Beneath the boughs, the shadows play,
As night descends and light gives way.
Curled ferns reveal a hidden truth,
In agile roots of ancient youth.

The moon casts silver on the glen,
While creatures stir beyond the fen.
Each footfall cautious, hearts attuned,
To mysteries that night has groomed.

With every twinkle high above,
The air's alive with silent love.
For in the veil where mysteries screen,
The whispers guide what's yet unseen.

So wander forth, embrace the riddle,
Let Nature's tune play softly, siddle.
In verdant veils, the truth prevails,
In enigmas wrapped in the night's tales.

Celestial Harmonies Amidst the Thickets

In thickets deep, the starlight weaves,
A tapestry where twilight breathes.
The whispers of the night take flight,
And dance among the trees so bright.

Beneath the moon's soft, silver glow,
The melodies of nightflowers flow.
Each note a secret, sweet and rare,
A song of magic fills the air.

The rustling leaves join in the tune,
As nature waltzes 'neath the moon.
In shadows cast, the dreams arise,
Invoking ancient lullabies.

Through branches thick, the stars peer down,
In whispers soft, they'll wear their crown.
In thickets dark, the world stands still,
As time surrenders to its will.

O let us drift on this soft breeze,
In harmony with rustling leaves.
For in this moment, all is right,
Celestial music fills the night.

The Enchanted Bower's Sigh

Within the bower, dreams take flight,
Where whispers linger, soft and light.
Petals drifting on a breeze,
Wrapped in nature's gentle ease.

The sunlight spills through leaves above,
A golden gift, a spark of love.
Each breeze a tale, each sigh a song,
Together where our hearts belong.

In this refuge, the world feels whole,
The magic wraps around the soul.
With every rustle, secrets shared,
In this bower, none feels ensnared.

So let us rest upon this ground,
Where kindness dwells and dreams abound.
In every shadow, hope is sown,
In this enchanted space, we've grown.

With twilight's hush, the stars ignite,
A tapestry of sheer delight.
In the bower's warm embrace we sigh,
As gentle echoes bid goodbye.

Tales of Wonder Beneath Ancient Boughs

Beneath the boughs, where shadows lie,
Whispers of wonder float and fly.
With every breeze, a tale unfolds,
Of ancient days and secrets old.

The roots entwined in earth's embrace,
Hold stories of our sacred place.
Where creatures dance and laughter rings,
And nature herself softly sings.

In tangled vines, the magic swells,
In hidden nooks, a story dwells.
The forest hums a timeless tune,
Beneath the watchful, quiet moon.

Each moment glimmers, truth entwined,
In every leaf, a spark of mind.
For in this realm, where magic dwells,
Are whispered lore and timeless spells.

And when the dusk descends on all,
The trees stand firm, they will not fall.
For tales of wonder, dreams, and sighs,
Live strong beneath these ancient skies.

Spirals of Mysticism in Nature

In spirals twine the roots and vines,
A dance within the grand designs.
Where every leaf holds wisdom dear,
In nature's song, we draw near.

The spirals weave through earth and sky,
In circles bright where spirits fly.
Each winding path a journey bold,
In echoes soft, the stories told.

The wind, a guide, through branches free,
Reveals the mystic's tapestry.
In every shadow, light is found,
Around us swirls the sacred sound.

With mindful steps, we tread the way,
Where nature hums and fairies play.
In swirls of magic, hearts unite,
As whispers beckon through the night.

Let us embrace this dance so true,
In spirals bright, we'll wander through.
For in each pulse of life we share,
Exists the mystic's tender care.

Fables from the Hidden Glen

In the glen where shadows dance,
Lies a tale of a stolen chance.
Whispers weave through leaves so green,
Secrets of the unseen queen.

Once a brooch of silver light,
Bound the fate of day and night.
With every flutter, fate would twine,
In the magic of the pine.

Creatures speak in riddled rhymes,
Hiding from the ticking times.
Echoes of the past live on,
In the quiet of the dawn.

By the brook where waters gleam,
Casting spells like a fleeting dream.
The air is thick with ancient lore,
And footsteps of those gone before.

So listen close as shadows play,
In the heart of the woodlands' sway.
For fables grow as stars ignite,
In the hush of the velvet night.

The Witching Hour's Embrace

When the clock strikes twelve with a sigh,
Magic stirs beneath the sky.
Shadows wrap about the trees,
Carried softly by the breeze.

Candles flicker, a spectral glow,
Whispers of the long ago.
In the hush, the secrets thrill,
The haunting dreams that linger still.

Midnight gathers, dreams take flight,
In the chime of silver light.
Wander tales through misty air,
In the realm of the midnight fair.

A spell is cast with moonlit charms,
Embracing all with open arms.
Listen closer, hear the call,
Of enchanted beings enthralled.

For in this hour, magic reigns,
In every heart, the longing gains.
So heed the call of night's sweet song,
In the witching hour, you belong.

Whims of the Wandering Spirits

Ghostly breezes, playful sighs,
Whimsical forms beneath the skies.
Dancing softly on the ground,
Where echoes of the lost are found.

With laughter light as frothy waves,
They flit between the hidden graves.
Stories swirl in twilight's glow,
As the moon crests high and low.

Each spirit holds a lingering quest,
Between the realms they find their rest.
Chasing wishes, they paint the air,
With dreams that linger, here and there.

Through silvered mists and laughter's tune,
They weave their magic 'neath the moon.
In the stillness, they leave their mark,
Guiding souls from light to dark.

So should you hear their gentle call,
In the whispers of the autumnal fall,
Join the dance, let your spirit fly,
To the whims of those who never die.

Beneath the Canopy of Whispers

Underneath the leafy crown,
Where sunlight dances, never frown.
Dreams are woven in the shade,
Where stories bend and never fade.

Silent songs from roots that creep,
In the soil, where secrets sleep.
Crickets sing and night winds sigh,
As shadows flicker, spirits fly.

Among the branches, a tale unfolds,
Of ancient magic, brave and bold.
Fairies flit, with laughter sweet,
Beneath the canopy, they meet.

Guided by the stars above,
They share a bond of endless love.
In every rustle, hear the plea,
Of nature's heart, wild and free.

So linger here, let moments pass,
In the emerald sea of grass.
For beneath the trees, life hums and sways,
In the whispers of the woods' embrace.

Dreamweaver's Lullaby in the Woods

In the hush of twilight's embrace,
Whispers of night begin their chase.
Stars blink gently in skies of blue,
While dreams weave softly, calling you.

Moonlight dances on leaves so fair,
Casting shadows, secrets laid bare.
A melody drifts on the breeze,
Crickets sing among the trees.

Close your eyes, let worries flee,
Nature's choir sings in glee.
In the woods where hopes take flight,
Find your peace in the still of night.

Starlit paths guide your way home,
Join the fae where the dreams roam.
With every breath, let magic bloom,
As slumber wraps you in its loom.

So breathe in deep, let magic stay,
In the quiet woods where dreams play.
When morning breaks, new dreams will find,
The heart that's open, the soul aligned.

Beneath the Canopy of Mystical Dreams

Under the arch of ancient trees,
Time drifts lightly, like the breeze.
Hushed whispers wrap the starlit dark,
Awakening each hidden spark.

Moonflowers bloom with silver light,
Guiding dreamers through the night.
Each shadow holds a tale untold,
A tapestry of dreams to unfold.

Walk softly on this enchanted ground,
Where laughter of sprites is sweetly found.
Beyond each brook and hidden glade,
Lies the magic that never fades.

In softest sighs and gentle laughter,
You'll find the dreams you're after.
Close your eyes, let the visions soar,
Beneath the trees, forevermore.

With every heartbeat, let hope grow,
In the mystic realm, let your spirit flow.
For dreams are born in every heart,
Beneath the canopy, life's true art.

The Shimmering World Beyond the Thorns

Through the thicket, a path unfolds,
Where secrets of the forest hold.
Glimmers dance in the twilight air,
Leading wanderers with tender care.

Every thorn a tale it brings,
Of forgotten songs and ancient kings.
With courage found in shadows deep,
The heart will guide where spirits leap.

Golden lights beckon from afar,
Whispers carried on moonlight's car.
Embrace the magic woven tight,
In every corner of dream-filled night.

Beyond the thorns, where dangers lie,
Hope emerges, soaring high.
Let your spirit rise and twirl,
In the shimmering world, let dreams unfurl.

So take a step, oh dreamer, bold,
Into the stories yet untold.
With every breath, find strength anew,
In the shimmering world waiting for you.

Glade of the Glimmering Spirits

In a glade where the soft winds sigh,
Whispers weave like clouds in the sky.
Where spirits flit with laughter bright,
And shadows dance in the pale moonlight.

Here, the flowers speak in hues,
Telling tales that may bemuse.
Each petal holds a wish or dream,
A glimmering thread in the night's seam.

Gentle breezes carry sweet scent,
From the hearts of the spirits, joyfully lent.
With each soft rustle, a secret shared,
In this glade, all souls are spared.

Close your eyes, feel the magic flow,
In this haven where new hopes grow.
Embrace the sights, let troubles cease,
In the glade of spirits, find your peace.

With laughter echoing in your heart,
Discover where the dreams impart.
For in this glade, the night is bright,
With spirits glimmering, a wondrous sight.

Veils of Mystery in the Elder Glade

In the glade where shadows creep,
Ancient whispers softly weep.
Moonlight dances on the trees,
Secrets swaying in the breeze.

A silver mist begins to rise,
Drawing near, the truth belies.
Every rustle sings the night,
Woven dreams blend dark with light.

Faded tales of those who roam,
In this place, they find a home.
With each step, enchantments bloom,
Treading paths where no one's groomed.

Glimmers spark in twilight's shroud,
Gather close, the spirits crowd.
Elder roots hold magic's grain,
In the glade, time veils the pain.

In the Heart of the Bewitched Thicket

Beneath the boughs of twisted vine,
Whispers echo, fate entwined.
Where enchanted creatures dwell,
Every shadow holds a spell.

Crimson flowers bloom and sway,
Markers for the lost who stray.
Through the thicket, secrets glide,
In the heart, where truths abide.

Golden sunlight streaks the floor,
Opening a crafted door.
Each leaf holds a tale untold,
In their veins, the magic's bold.

Listen close, the night will sing,
To the air, let wishes cling.
Bewitched thicket holds the key,
To the dreams that long to be.

Twisting Branches and Hidden Spells

Twisting branches arch and weave,
Guarding dreams that none believe.
In the silence, soft and sweet,
Magic's pulse can feel the beat.

Hushed are birds on whispered wings,
Nature cradles ancient things.
With each rustle, the air turns still,
Every thought begins to thrill.

Under stars that flicker bright,
Mysteries dance within the night.
Hidden spells lace through the trees,
Drawing close the spirits' pleas.

Wanderers treading light and slow,
Follow paths where rivers flow.
In the shadows, treasures hide,
Twisting branches, time's true guide.

Secrets of the Wildwood Canopy

High above in leafy green,
Whispers weave, a gentle screen.
Sunlit beams and shadows play,
Secrets cradle night and day.

Listen well to rustling leaves,
Every branch the wildwood weaves.
Clouds drift softly, secrets share,
Floating dreams lost in the air.

Mossy stones and gnarled roots,
Echo tales of magic's pursuits.
Faeries dance on moonlit trails,
In the woods, where wonder hails.

Dappled light through branches spills,
Kisses each with gentle thrills.
Secrets linger in twilight's coat,
In the silence, hearts will float.

A Spellbook of the Natural Realm

In whispers of the ancient trees,
A spellbook waits in rustling leaves,
With ink of night and quills of light,
It tells the tales that nature weaves.

Each page adorned with shimmering brume,
Of fairies and sprites in magic's bloom,
They dance in circles, casting their charms,
With secrets held in nature's arms.

The rivers murmur, the mountains sing,
While creatures gather, enchantments bring,
The wisdom of soil, the grace of the sky,
In every heartbeat, the wild things sigh.

With every page the world unfolds,
Of hidden magic that life beholds,
A journey begun with each gentle turn,
In the spellbook's truths, our spirits burn.

So wander softly, attune your heart,
Let nature's whispers be your art,
For in the realm where shadows play,
The spellbook's secrets light the way.

Revelations Within the Enchanted Thicket

In thickets lush, where shadows dwell,
Revelations bloom like a silent bell,
The rustling leaves hold stories untold,
Of fae and fortune, both young and old.

A veil of mist, so soft and pale,
Threads through the trees, a whispered tale,
Of dreams awakened in twilight's grace,
In every corner, a hidden place.

With each step taken on the mossy ground,
New wonders breathe, new truths are found,
The song of night spills from feathered throats,
In the heart of night, enchantment floats.

The thicket pulses with vibrant life,
A sanctuary free from worldly strife,
Where wishes twinkle like fireflies bright,
In the embrace of the soft moonlight.

So linger long, let your spirit roam,
Within this realm, you'll find your home,
For every thicket holds a spark,
A revelation born from shadowed dark.

The Elfin Melody of Moonlit Thorns

Within the thorns where moonbeams play,
An elfin melody drifts away,
It dances softly on the night breeze,
Carried by whispers of rustling leaves.

With every note, a secret unveiled,
Of heart and hope, where dreams have sailed,
Through tangled woods adorned with stars,
Each sound a glimpse of life's memoirs.

The thorns, though sharp, hold beauty true,
In shadows cast, the magic grew,
Their whispers twine 'neath silver skies,
Where elves weave spells and laughter flies.

A symphony of night's sweet songs,
Of whispered truths and ancient wrongs,
They harmonize in softest hues,
Painting the darkness with rainbow views.

So pause a while, lend ear to the sound,
In moonlit thorns, your soul is bound,
For every melody, a heart reborn,
In the elfin night, a new world is formed.

Fleeing Shadows and Luminous Wands

In flickering dusk, the shadows flee,
While luminous wands weave spells with glee,
They dance upon a canvas of night,
Crafting dreams in a flickering light.

The air is thick with magic's breath,
A pulse of life that conquers death,
With every flick, a tale ignites,
As wand tips sparkle, revealing sights.

Shadows whisper of fears to unveil,
Yet wands respond with a fiery trail,
Each movement bold, a promise made,
To chase the night with vibrant shade.

Flee, oh shadows, into the deep,
For light awakens where magic leaps,
In every heart, a spark will ignite,
A luminous wonder to conquer the night.

So grasp your wand, let courage rise,
Defy the dark with radiant skies,
For in the dance of shadows and light,
A new adventure begins tonight.

Twilight's Spellbound Oracles

In twilight's grasp, where shadows blend,
The whispered tales of wizards wend.
Through glades adorned with silvery light,
Starlit beings dance, a magical sight.

With every breath, an oath is sworn,
To heed the stars where dreams are born.
Beneath the arch of emerald trees,
Secrets unfold upon the breeze.

The oracle's gaze, both wise and deep,
Holds the fates of those who sleep.
In runes and signs, the truth is spun,
A tapestry filled with battles won.

In echoes soft, the ancients call,
Their cryptic words, a lingering thrall.
You hear them whispered in the night,
Guiding lost souls toward the light.

So linger here, 'neath starry skies,
And delve into this world of lies.
For every heart that dares to seek,
Finds in twilight, magic unique.

Tales of the Arcane Thicket

In verdant thickets, shadows play,
Where secrets dwell, and lost dreams stay.
The rustling leaves, a subtle tune,
Mysteries draped in afternoon.

A flicker here, a whisper there,
Bewitched by nature's softest air.
Arcane echoes stir the trees,
Unraveling spells in every breeze.

Fragments of lore in twilight gleam,
As sprites weave freely, hearts in dream.
The moon casts down a silver veil,
Guiding the lost along the trail.

With every step, the magic grows,
Through tangled woods where wildflowers pose.
Each petal holds a tale to tell,
Of journeys far, through time's vast swell.

So wander deep, where few have gone,
In every shadow, a spark of dawn.
For in the thicket's embrace you'll find,
The hidden wonders unfurling, unconfined.

The Gloom of Sundering Leaves

Amidst the forest, shadows loom,
Where nature's whispers spell its gloom.
Leaves once bright, now tinged with gray,
In autumn's grip, they drift away.

Beneath the boughs, old echoes sigh,
Of days gone by that never die.
Their stories linger, bittersweet,
In hollow trunks and at our feet.

The fading light that dims the day,
Holds shards of dusk in disarray.
With every rustle, memories blend,
Of love and loss that night will send.

As twilight drapes the world in blue,
The silence speaks, both bold and true.
Each falling leaf, a tale untold,
In nature's arms, we find our hold.

So tread with care through sorrowed ground,
For in the quiet, magic's found.
And from the gloom, new life will rise,
Beneath the stars, beyond the skies.

Murmurs of Ancient Enchantment

In moonlit groves where shadows weave,
The ancient whispers never leave.
Songs of old, like mist, arise,
Enchanted dreams that mesmerize.

A rustle here, a flicker there,
The world transformed by magic's flair.
With every step, the secrets call,
In echoes soft, we heed their thrall.

In runes and marks, the wisdom waits,
Unlocking all the hidden gates.
Each talisman, a heart's desire,
Ignites within a flickering fire.

As starlight kisses the night so fair,
Magic dances in the air.
The murmurs swirl, a sweet refrain,
Of ancient times and dreams regained.

So listen close, as night descends,
For in the dark, the spirit bends.
To guide the lost, to spark delight,
In ancient songs of stillness, light.

Enchanted Breezes Through the Grove

In the glade where shadows dance,
Whispers weave through leaves' romance.
Glimmers twinkle in the dusk,
A secret song, a fragrant musk.

Laughter flits on fairy wings,
Jubilant notes that nature sings.
Winds that carry tales untold,
In the heart of woods, pure gold.

Mossy stones in twilight's beam,
Crystals glisten, dreams take theme.
Softly glows the moonlit haze,
Bathing all in silver praise.

Legends echo through the night,
In moonlit paths, a mystic sight.
Each footstep stirs the sleeping ground,
Magic's pulse is all around.

As stars peep through the canopy,
They watch o'er us in harmony.
Enchanted breezes swirl and play,
Guiding souls on their lost way.

The Wishing Whisper of Gnarled Boughs

Beneath boughs twisted and wise,
In silence, secrets softly rise.
A wish hangs on the forest air,
Heavy with dreams and gentle care.

With every crack of a worn limb,
Shadows echo when the light dims.
Faintly calls a voice, so sweet,
Guiding wanderers on their feet.

Gnarled roots hold forgotten lore,
A tapestry of tales galore.
Each gentle sway, a story spun,
Of battles fought and victories won.

Creeks that glimmer like stars in flight,
Reflect the hopes of day and night.
Every rustle of leaves attest,
The whispers keep the heart at rest.

So listen close with open heart,
The gnarled boughs play their part.
In the stillness, find your way,
The wishes bloom and gently sway.

Murmurs of The Twilight Garden

In gardens where the shadows creep,
The twilight sings, the world's asleep.
Petals fold with secrets held,
In fragrant notes, the dreams are spelled.

Starlight blinks through ivy's embrace,
A celestial dance in hidden space.
Murmurs drift on perfumed air,
Promises linger, soft and rare.

Whispers flow from blooms so bright,
Casting spells in the fading light.
Each color breathes, a living tale,
Of summer's dusk and autumn's veil.

Evening's brush paints everything,
Gold and violet, a gentle string.
Nature bows in a soft refrain,
As shadows weave through joy and pain.

In this haven of dusk-time dreams,
The garden hums in whispered themes.
Murmurs float like morning dew,
A twilight's song, forever true.

Secrets of the Twisted Elders

Around the elders, branches twist,
In silent watch, they co-exist.
Time's own keepers, wise and grand,
Guarding secrets of the land.

Each knot and curve, a tale invoked,
Through centuries of life, bespoke.
Voices echo from bark and leaf,
Fables forged in joy and grief.

Mossy cloaks cover ancient bark,
Sheltering treasures in the dark.
Roots entwined in a dark embrace,
Hold the essence of this place.

With every breeze that passes by,
The elders whisper, never shy.
Secrets shared with every sigh,
Of love lost and dreams awry.

So pause and listen, heart aligned,
In nature's depths, true peace you'll find.
The twisted elders guide us near,
In every heart, their voices clear.

Chronicles Beneath the Canopy

In emerald halls where whispers dwell,
The ancient trees weave tales to tell.
Beneath their shade, the secrets lie,
Of realms forgotten, time drifts by.

A wanderer's heart, in shadows cast,
Seeks paths of light, but holds the past.
With every breath, the stories hum,
In rustling leaves, the echoes come.

A single ray through branches breaks,
Awakens dreams the forest makes.
In twilight's glow, spirits arise,
To dance among the starry skies.

The moon above, a watchful eye,
Guides the brave who dare to fly.
In every root and every bough,
Lie tales of yore, both fierce and foul.

So take a step and heed the call,
For magic breathes within it all.
In every rustle, every sigh,
The Chronicles will never die.

Serpentines of Sorcery

In shadows deep where secrets weave,
Serpentines of sorcery, we believe.
The flicker of a wand, a whispered name,
A spark ignites the ancient flame.

Beneath the moon, the potions brew,
Midnight's elixir, sought by few.
The flickering candles cast their spell,
In the heart of darkness, all is well.

A cauldron bubbles with dreams of night,
As fate's cruel hand finds wrong or right.
With every incantation, shadows play,
Lost in the dance of night and day.

With serpentine grace, the magic flows,
In every twist, the power grows.
Weaving the threads of fate so fine,
Within this realm, our spirits entwine.

So cast your gaze upon the stars,
And forge your path, despite the scars.
For in the mystic, truth will find,
The heart's desire, once confined.

Embrace of the Gnarled Roots

In twilight's glow beneath the trees,
The gnarled roots whisper in the breeze.
They cradle secrets of ages past,
In their embrace, the shadows cast.

A child of earth, with tangled hair,
Drawn to the wild, beyond compare.
With every step, the forest sighs,
In harmony, the old voice cries.

The dance of nature, a sacred rite,
Beneath the moon's soft, silver light.
Where wildflowers bloom in muted grace,
And time stands still in this enchanted place.

The roots extend where stories dwell,
Like echoes of a long-lost bell.
A heart that listens will surely find,
The magic woven, intertwined.

So hold the earth in tender clasp,
And let the ancient wisdom grasp.
The gnarled roots will gladly share,
The truth of life, beyond despair.

Rituals of the Midnight Shift

When shadows stretch and the clock strikes twelve,
The midnight shift unfolds itself.
In hidden corners, whispers creep,
Where secrets linger, dark and deep.

The flicker of candle, sharp with fate,
Marks the hour when dreams await.
With patient hands, the rituals start,
In the stillness, both fierce and art.

Incantations flow like silver streams,
Awakening the heart's wild dreams.
In realms unseen, they weave and spin,
A tapestry of loss and win.

So gather round, the chosen few,
In midnight's embrace, the bond is true.
With every breath, the magic swells,
In silent whispers, the story dwells.

As stars align in darkened skies,
In the quiet, the spirit flies.
From dusk till dawn, the shift will lend,
A doorway where the shadows blend.

Veils of Mist Over Hallowed Ground

In the morning hush, the fog descends,
Softly veiling where the earth extends.
Ancient trees stand like silent guards,
Whispering secrets in forgotten yards.

Footsteps echo on the dew-kissed grass,
Moments linger as the shadows pass.
Veils of mist dance with ghostly grace,
Hallowed ground holds time in its embrace.

A glimmer of light breaks through the gray,
Guiding the brave who dare to stay.
With every breath, the magic swells,
Stories awaken where the magic dwells.

Crimson leaves spiral in the breeze,
Carrying tales from the time of trees.
Under the arch of a weeping vine,
The heart of the forest beats divine.

Here, in the stillness, spirits convene,
In the realm where the air feels keen.
Veils of mist, a serene shroud,
Protecting dreams beneath the cloud.

The Forest's Heartbeat and Spellbound Paths

In twilight's glow, the forest sighs,
Whispers mingling with starry skies.
A treasure trove of magic untold,
Awakens secrets from ages old.

Footsteps wander, a gentle trace,
Through spellbound paths, a wild embrace.
Each rustling leaf sings of delight,
In the throbbing pulse of the night.

Beneath the boughs, the spirits play,
Carving laughter into the day.
Starlit shadows dance and sway,
As moonlit visions come out to play.

An echoing call beckons the bold,
To chase the wonders yet untold.
Magic flows in whispers and dreams,
Like shimmering threads in silver streams.

With every step, the forest breathes,
Woven stories in silent wreaths.
A heartbeat thrums, alive and wise,
Where nature's magic never dies.

Echoes of Enchantment in the Clearing

In the clearing, a song is spun,
Beneath the gaze of the setting sun.
Echoes of laughter, bright and clear,
Dancing on winds that draw us near.

Mirth and shadows twine like lace,
In this enchanted, sacred place.
Every whisper, a tale reborn,
As twilight drapes the world in morn.

With sparkling eyes, the stars align,
While the moon bestows its silver sign.
In the heart of magic, hope takes flight,
Woven dreams unfold in shimmering light.

Creatures of legend flit about,
Jubilant songs are what they're about.
In every rustle and whispered phrase,
A tapestry of wondrous days.

So linger long in this gentle glow,
Breathe in the wonders, let them flow.
In the clearing, where enchantment lies,
Life spills forth in a cascade of sighs.

In Pursuit of Wandering Whispers

In dusky twilight, shadows blend,
Whispers beckon, as night ascends.
Through winding paths, the stories roam,
In pursuit of whispers that call us home.

Each flickering light, a guide anew,
Leading hearts to secrets true.
Threads of silver weave through the dark,
A song of the night—a hidden spark.

With every footstep, the world shifts light,
Magic unfurling in the depths of night.
The air is thick with dreams to chase,
In this enchanted, timeless space.

Every breeze carries echoing lore,
As ancient spirits dance evermore.
In pursuit we tread, seeking and finding,
The pulse of magic, resounding, binding.

Cloaked in wonder, the night draws near,
In between whispers, we shed our fear.
For in the tales that the night confides,
The heart of the world forever abides.

Enfolded in the Olives of Enchantment

In groves where sunlight softly falls,
The olives dance, as nature calls.
With every breeze, a secret shared,
In whispers sweet, the heart is bared.

A twilight glow, the branches sway,
Inviting souls to stay and play.
The silver leaves, they shimmer bright,
Enfolding dreams in soft, warm light.

Each shadow holds a story spun,
Of magic lost and battles won.
With every step, the past unfolds,
In every sigh, the truth is told.

Beneath the boughs, the silence hums,
A melody from twilight drums.
Embrace the peace, let worries flee,
For in the grove, the soul is free.

So linger here, in nature's grace,
And find the joy in this sweet place.
For life is but a fleeting spark,
Enfolded in the evening's dark.

Moondust Trails in Mystic Delights

Beneath the glow of silver moons,
We wander paths to hidden tunes.
With twinkling stars to guide our way,
In secret nooks where fairies play.

The night unfolds a velvet cover,
As dreams awake and spirits hover.
With every step, the magic swirls,
In whispered plots, the mystery twirls.

A cascade of light on whispered trails,
Where ancient song and silence sails.
With every breath, the moment sings,
In gentle nooks where the magic clings.

Dance with shadows, light and free,
Let the moon weave its tapestry.
In every heart, a spark ignites,
On moondust trails in mystic nights.

So chase the dreams as dawn appears,
And let them lead through laughter's tears.
For in each step, a story grows,
In mystic delights, the magic flows.

Cloaked in the Whispers of the Grove

In twilight's kiss, the world retreats,
Where silence wraps the heart's soft beats.
Cloaked in shadows, secrets thrive,
In whispered breath, the shadows drive.

Boughs entwined, with stories shared,
In every leaf, a heart is bared.
The rustle soft, like dreams that call,
In quiet peace, we rise or fall.

The nightingale sings to the moon so bright,
Guiding lost souls through endless night.
With every song, the spirits rise,
In hidden realms beyond our eyes.

With hands outstretched, we feel the warmth,
Of ancient souls, a gentle charm.
Cloaked in the whispers, dreams take flight,
In the quiet grove, we find our light.

So linger long in the forest deep,
And let the magic hold you, keep.
For in each sigh, a wonder stirs,
Cloaked in the grove where silence purrs.

A Song for the Forgotten Glade

In the heart of woods where shadows blend,
A melody calls, a spirit's friend.
In the forgotten glade, time stands still,
As nature weaves its gentle thrill.

The flowers bloom with tender grace,
Painting the air with their soft embrace.
With every note, the heart takes flight,
In the hush of twilight, pure delight.

A stream whispers secrets to the trees,
Carried on winds that dance with ease.
In the glade's cocoon, we find our song,
For in this place, we all belong.

As fireflies twinkle in soft ballet,
The night unfolds in a magical play.
With every breath, the universe sways,
In the song that lingers, dusk to rays.

So listen close with an open heart,
To whispers of wisdom that grace this art.
For in the glade, our souls entwine,
A song for the ages, forever divine.

Spheres of Enchantment in Cobalt Skies

In the heart of the night, under sapphire gleams,
Whispers of magic dance in silvery streams.
Stars weave their tales in celestial flight,
Binding the dreamers to the veil of night.

Winds carry secrets through the deep azure,
Soft with a promise, each breath is a lure.
Mysteries shimmer in the starlit glow,
Echoes of wonders that time cannot slow.

Crystals of hope in the depths of the shade,
Awaken the spirits, the fears they invade.
With flickers of light, they rise and they play,
Filling the darkness, then fading away.

Lunar reflections on tranquil seas,
Murmur to hearts like the softest of pleas.
In the vast cobalt, truths long lost remain,
Spheres of enchantment, where dreams break the chain.

Along the Path of Mysterious Bloom

Beneath twilight's gaze, where shadows entwine,
Petals unfurl their secrets divine.
Shimmering colors dance under the moon,
Awakening spirits with an ancient tune.

Whispers of blooms murmur stories of old,
Of love and of loss, the brave and the bold.
Along hidden paths, where light gently weaves,
Enchanting illusions drift on autumn leaves.

The air holds a fragrance, both rich and profound,
As blooms unveil wonders from deep underground.
Nature's sweet treasures, so lush and so bright,
Awaken the senses in the heart of the night.

In gardens unseen, where dreams start to soar,
Each flower a wish, opening wide every door.
Mysteries murmur, as starlight ascends,
Along the soft path, where enchantment never ends.

Realm of Shadows and Celestial Blooms

In the realm of shadows, where twilight sings,
Celestial blooms unfold wondrous wings.
Veils of the cosmos drape over the land,
Crafting illusions by nature's own hand.

Each petal a gleam from the heavens above,
Whispers of fate weave through threads of love.
Stars glance down, with a knowing delight,
In the dance of the dark and the kiss of the light.

Flutters of creatures with magic bestowed,
Roam through the night, on enchantment they rode.
With shadows as allies, they swirl and they dive,
In a realm where the dreamers are truly alive.

Eclipses of moments, where dreams intertwine,
A garden of wonder, both tender and fine.
With shadows a canvas, and stars shining bright,
Celestial blooms flourish in the heart of the night.

The Sorceress's Lair Among the Boughs

High in the branches, where secrets are spun,
Dwells a sorceress; her spells softly run.
Among ancient oaks, where shadows cascade,
She nurtures the magic, in stillness arrayed.

With flickering candles and whispers of lore,
Her heart beats in time with the roots evermore.
Potions and charms in a glow softly stir,
As nature's own heartbeat whispers to her.

The leaves share their stories, the wind brings a song,
Echoing secrets that linger so long.
In her lair of wonder, the unseen takes flight,
Awakening dreams in the cloak of the night.

Beneath her soft gaze, the world spins and charms,
With spells that enchant, and nature that warms.
Bridges of magic, weaving tales from above,
In the sorceress's lair, we discover our love.

Whispers of Enchanted Glades

In glades where twilight softly hums,
The magic glimmers, never succumbs.
With ivy's embrace, dreams entwine,
Where echoes of laughter and whispers align.

Beneath the trees, with bark so wise,
They tell of wonders beneath the skies.
Fairies dance where the wildflowers grow,
Secrets unfurl in the evening's glow.

The moon spills silver on tranquil streams,
Where starlit waters cradle sweet dreams.
Each rustle and sigh, a story retold,
In the heart of the forest, a treasure of gold.

Glimmers of hope nestle in the leaves,
Where every breath a new magic weaves.
Under the canopy, time drifts like mist,
In whispers of glades, we find what we've missed.

So wander the paths where the shadows play,
Embrace the marvels that linger and stay.
For in every step, the enchantment is found,
In whispers of glades, pure joy does abound.

Secrets of the Mystic Grove

Deep in the woods where secrets hide,
The heart of the grove sings soft and wide.
A tapestry woven of dusk and lore,
Whispers of magic at the forest's core.

With mossy trails that twine and weave,
The past and present together believe.
Cloaked in the mist, the ancients listen,
To tales untold where the starlight glisten.

In twilight's embrace, shadows extend,
In silence, the spirits of nature descend.
Each rustling leaf holds a tale of yore,
Secrets unfold as the night starts to soar.

Beneath the boughs where the night owls dwell,
A chorus of crickets begins to swell.
Glimpse the unseen, don't fear the unknown,
For within these whispers, enchantment is sown.

So venture forth into this mystic place,
Where secrets and solace weave a warm lace.
With every heartbeat, you'll come to find,
The magic of the grove forever entwined.

Twisted Boughs Under Moonlight

Beneath the moon's watchful, silver gaze,
Twisted boughs twist in a delicate maze.
The night air thickens with the scent of pine,
Where secrets dwell and starlight aligns.

Each gnarled branch a keeper of tales,
Of whispered wishes on unseen trails.
In the stillness, the world softly sighs,
As shadows awaken beneath the skies.

Glow of the moonlight, a ghostly light,
Illuminates paths where day turns to night.
The forest breathes, a living dream,
In the glow of the night, all wonder streams.

With every rustle, a legend unfolds,
In the arms of the trees, where magic beholds.
The chime of the crickets, a melodic tune,
Lingers in hearts like the warmest afternoon.

So wander these woods under moon's embrace,
With twisted boughs, find your rightful place.
For here in the shadows, your spirit will soar,
In the silence of night, there's so much in store.

Shadows of the Forest's Heart

In shadows deep, where the silence sleeps,
The forest heart a secret keeps.
With every heartbeat of ancient trees,
Whispers rise in the gentle breeze.

Where wild blooms kiss the forest floor,
Tender petals that softly implore.
In the dusk, where the day meets the night,
The world stands still, wrapped in twilight's light.

Mysterious paths lead to unknown realms,
Guided by spirits at nature's helm.
The dance of the fireflies, soft and bright,
Carrying dreams on the wings of night.

In glimmers of light, legends are drawn,
By the whispers of night, a new day is born.
So roam through the shadows, let your heart see,
The magic that lives, wild and free.

For in every shadow, a story awaits,
In the forest's heart, where destiny baits.
With every step, let your spirit take flight,
For shadows of dreams weave a wondrous night.

Tales from the Winding Bramble

In a glade where shadows weave,
The bramble whispers tales of eve.
Through tangled roots, the magic hums,
And secrets bloom where wild things come.

The moonlit path, a silver thread,
Where creatures dart and dreams are fed.
Each rustling leaf, a spell to cast,
Making memories of the past.

Beneath the boughs, old stories sigh,
Of forgotten hopes that wandered by.
The bramble's heart holds dreams untold,
In colors bright, and shades of gold.

Here, friendships blossom, fears are tossed,
In the dance of light, no soul is lost.
Heart to heart, and hand in hand,
Together we weave this enchanted land.

So heed the sounds of bramble's call,
For magic sings, entwining all.
A winding path, where wonders gleam,
In the heart of the wild, we dare to dream.

By Starlit Glimmers and Gossamer Dreams

Beneath the vast and velvet sky,
The stars like lanterns gently sigh.
In glimmers bright, the night's embrace,
We chase the dreams that time can't trace.

With gossamer threads spun of night,
We weave our hopes in soft moonlight.
Each breath a wish upon the breeze,
Carried away through ancient trees.

In whispers sweet, the cosmos weaves,
The tapestry of all our believes.
O'er shimmering streams, where fairies dance,
In starlit glades, we take our chance.

The secrets held by skies afar,
Illuminate our guiding star.
Through twilight's kiss, we softly glide,
In realms where shadows gently bide.

So venture forth, let spirits soar,
By starlit glimmers, we'll seek for more.
In gossamer dreams, we find our way,
Embracing night, welcoming day.

The Enchantress's Secret Refuge

In a garden where wild roses twine,
An enchantress serves her potent wine.
With herbs and roots, her cauldron simmers,
In flickering light, the shadows glimmer.

The air is rich with a fragrant spell,
As stories of old in whispers dwell.
Hidden beneath the yew tree's shade,
Lies the magic that never fades.

Her refuge sings of quiet grace,
In every corner, a secret space.
The moonlit pond reflects her dreams,
A mirror of hope surrounded by beams.

With hands that craft both love and pain,
She conquers loss, she wields the rain.
Through trials faced, her spirit bends,
In this haven, the heart transcends.

So come and seek her whispered song,
In the refuge where the lost belong.
An enchantress waits with open arms,
To share the depth of her charmed charms.

A Dance with the Elders of the Forest

In the heart of the forest deep,
The ancient elders wake from sleep.
With twisted limbs and knowing eyes,
They guard the earth where magic lies.

A rustling leaf, a whispered rhyme,
In echoes soft, they dance through time.
Beneath the boughs, the music swells,
In every heartbeat, a tale compels.

The shadows sway, the moonlight glows,
As wisdom flows where the wild wind blows.
With every step, the earth does sigh,
A dance of life that cannot die.

So join the waltz, embrace the night,
With nurturing darkness, find the light.
In unity, the forest beams,
A timeless bond born of the dreams.

Together we weave through ancient trees,
In the elders' grace, find our ease.
A dance that promises a world reborn,
In harmony with the dew-kissed dawn.